Every household is different and has different needs. The information in this handbook is the opinion of the author and is intended only as suggestions.

Copyright © 2023 Dana L.C. Miller

All rights reserved.

Paperback: 979-8-218-16426-3

Edited by Jodi Cecil

Letter From the Author

Welcome! Tech safety for our kids is such an important topic to address early and often. This handbook is here for exactly that reason: to help make it manageable and approachable. You are busy, and even taking the time to read a short handbook says so much about your commitment to your household's online safety.

My background is in the law enforcement and education fields. I am a former part of the Internet Crimes Against Children (ICAC) Task Force, which provided me many years of opportunities to help children that were being manipulated and abused, and which supplied me the expertise to bring this information to parents and guardians with a goal of preventing exploitation. The ICAC Task Force is a national task force that specializes in combatting online child exploitation, and you'll see I refer to ICAC throughout the handbook. The work they do is amazing!

A large part of that work, and one I refer to a few times throughout, deals with CyberTips from the National Center for Missing & Exploited Children (NCMEC)'s CyberTipline. The CyberTipline is the nation's centralized reporting system for online exploitation of children, and the number of reports they receive each year increases at an alarming rate. As you read, you'll find that I rarely refer to specific statistics. I chose this format because technology changes so rapidly, as does our children's use of it, that I thought it best to focus on the information instead of the current statistics which may quickly become outdated. I do share resources for current research in the Resource Ideas & Tools section at the end of the handbook, but we can sum it up with this:

Both NCMEC and the ICAC Task Force are far busier than we want them to be.

My hope is that you'll be the trusted person your child comes to if they need help. And beyond that, my sincere hope is that we can reach a point where no child ever finds themselves in a situation where they are being exploited or need that help. Thanks for taking the time for this information and for having these very important conversations with your child. Let's talk early and often.

Stay safe,
Dana Miller

Table of contents

Chapter 1 | Technology: From Toddlers to Teens……………………………………………5

Chapter 2 | Stack 'em up! Building Blocks for Online Safety………………………….11

Chapter 3 | 8 Going on 18: So They Want a Device……………………………………….22

Chapter 4 | So They Want Social Media………………………………………………………28

Chapter 5 | Reducing Risky Behavior…………………………………………………………36

Chapter 6 | Responses & Resources……………………………………………………………47

Resource Ideas & Tools to Use…………………………………………………………………49

Chapter 1
Technology: From Toddlers to Teens

My barely over-one toddler could open my phone. My smartphone. My password-protected, *very expensive* smartphone. And in case you think it was a fluke…it was not. She got it unlocked regularly whenever those sticky (and I mean that both literally and figuratively) little fingers found my phone within reach on a table.

At least I can rest assured that she, like so many of our children, will probably have a great future in the tech realm. Regardless of your child's age, this story probably sounds at least somewhat familiar. I share some of my personal experiences with a toddler through this first chapter, as it is important for us to start talking about internet safety at any age we're able to incorporate it. If you haven't started yet, that's okay! Because what's most important is that you are looking for ways to start the conversation now.

If you are anything like me, you've given up already on having a phone with a clean, unbroken screen. It's just one of the many realities of parenthood – for me, anyway. The fact is, all kids have great interest in screens! I've worked in online safety and education for a long time. I know that every household is different, and the access children are given to technology – and when – varies from family to family, with good reason. I honestly never considered the details about how I would introduce my child to technology, I just knew I would start introducing tech safety as early as possible, too. Now I'm figuring out what that means in day-to-day life, a much larger feat than when I provide bullet point ideas during short presentations.

So, for my parent friends out there saying, "I don't need online safety yet, my child's only…." (*fill in the blank with whatever reason you've got*), let me recommend this: Let's start before we need it. Start incorporating small online use discussions and appropriate limits or safety into whatever your child is doing with technology. Why? Well, it's easier if you start early. It will become a natural part of how you and your child communicate regarding technology, and hopefully it will make your life easier with some already-set expectations of rules and limits. I've also found that this is a great time for me to re-evaluate my own relationship with my phone. I want to set a good example for my children about how I use and interact with technology, and part of that is limiting my own use. I've found countless times where I'll look up from my phone and will see my toddler watching me, which has led to me actively (and guiltily) putting my phone aside when I'm with her. My emails and scrolling can absolutely wait. I try to encourage this with the other adults in her life, as well, because technology use and having to "keep up" can often come with a mental health price. To be practical, we don't know where our children will interact with technology. My child spends some time with her grandparents, she goes to storytime at the library, and while all of that is still supervised, there will come a time when she is with friends or at school and the supervision is lessened. I want to be prepared for her interacting online before it happens, so that our discussions can grow with her tech use, and I don't have to try to play catchup when she's in grade school or middle school – with potentially more difficult safety conversations.

Let's talk about what this realistically means. Do I try to tell my toddler about online safety? Definitely not. She doesn't interact online yet, plus, she can't sit still for more than six seconds. But the phone she manages to swipe over and over again IS connected to the internet, and I'd prefer she not get into it and subscribe me to some unnecessary service, or text (or worse, *call*) a boss or one of those contacts you keep in your phone just to know not to answer! (Admit it, we all have them). Anyway, one way that I've started to incorporate it is to 'play' phone with her. She enjoys pretending to make or receive phone calls with the phone pressed to her ear - the other day she said she was calling our dog on the phone. This is much more fun (for me) than interacting with the screen, and I want her to know that we can have fun with technology while also having rules or limits. I talk to her about being 'gentle' or careful with my phone when she has it. Granted, this is partly selfish because I don't want to pay for yet another screen protector, but I think it's a good and easy way to start putting some sort of age-appropriate responsibility and limits on tech. We also make sure to put the phones away as often as possible. "That's enough looking at pictures for right now," with a redirect to some other fun activity is another option we use because she loves looking at pictures on our phones.

If these seem too easy, they should! They are all easy ways to start introducing limits and safety with tech – and that's the point. We just need to start, and <u>you are probably already doing it</u> without realizing it. Thinking about checking in on what they are doing or interested in, or talking about why limits are important, can help make those conversations consistent and part of your building blocks for safety. It also makes it easier to have future conversations as their tech use advances.

I cringe to say this, but we did also provide our toddler with her 'own phone' to play with already. It's an old flip phone that has no service, but she can swipe the screen and it reacts and provides the response that she's looking for. We have turned the airplane mode on, hoping to thwart her re-instating service since she's apparently a tech expert, and we've also turned the Voice Assistant on. She gets an audible response to her swipes and actions, and we can tell what she is doing with the phone since it announces everything. Giving a child an old device is a common action we hear from parents, and obviously, it makes sense! You might find yourself doing this with different-aged children, too. They can play games, interact safely with technology, and we can get dinner made or have a few minutes in peace during a car trip. I want to bring a few thoughts up for consideration, because there are safety concerns with everything. You should be informed so you can determine the best decisions for your household – some of these items won't matter to you, and that's just fine – remember, your rules are the right rules for your family.

Devices without service can still be connected to the internet via wifi. This may be how your child is playing games or watching videos, so this might not be news to you. However, it is important to remember that if they're on wifi, they can download apps and games from the app store, and many of those apps and games provide communication options with other users. For kids that are a bit older, they'll probably know that they can download apps that can provide their phone with a phone number, which then can be used to create some of those apps that might be age-inappropriate for young kids. We'll talk in future chapters about parental approvals, but in this case, just making sure the app downloads are locked or notifications are on for the account on that phone can help manage this concern. You can then look into that app/game and have discussions with your child or remove that app, if needed. (On a related note, also make sure that your in-app purchases are locked and voice purchases are locked on any voice-activated or smart speaker devices. It's always funny to read about people with huge dollhouses or grosses of cookie boxes delivered to their home when their child voice-orders online...until it's *your* child doing the ordering).

Another 'old device' consideration for awareness: many kids are using YouTube on a very frequent basis. Is your child posting to YouTube, as well? One thing we commonly saw in my work with the Internet Crimes Against Children (ICAC) Task Force was that kids would take videos of themselves doing things they thought were silly, like pulling down their pants. They don't mean anything by it, but for whatever reason, they might post those videos (or they might upload to cloud-photo storage). The account that device is assigned to is likely your (adult) account, and those platforms must report anything that appears to be online child exploitation on their platforms. Law enforcement will then be looking at you, the adult, as their suspect until they determine that it was just a child posting and only a safety talk is needed. If that isn't great incentive to have safety conversations with your kids about what to post and what *not* to post, I don't know what is!

Alright, but phones are only part of the problem, correct? Healthy screen time limits are the main place where tech limits have come in for our family so far with a young child. And as with everything, it would have been way easier if we would have started with these limits instead of trying to enforce them now that our toddler has been introduced to instant gratification of streaming. We often tell her that we'll watch two shows (and then let her watch two short videos/songs), or that, "Sometimes there are commercials, we just have to watch what's on." I read about a parent that started this with a pre-K child and explained that the shows were made to make us want to keep watching shows, and more shows means less fun time with mom and dad, or less fun time outside, or whatever the comparable is. The parent then asked the child how many shows they thought were the right number of shows, and when the child said two, they both felt like it was a win! As the child got a bit older, they started to negotiate; for example, the child offered to give up Thursday shows to be able to watch a Saturday movie. We will definitely be trying this when our child gets a bit older. Another idea we've tried is to use 'tickets' for an amount of television time. I've read that starting with toddler ages, you can determine the appropriate number of tickets for the day for your household and use this to remind us to pay a bit more attention to the amount of screentime and help set those limits. She picked it up very quickly but we didn't use it for long – it just wasn't 'the ticket' (get it?) for our household. I know we'll find other new ideas to try as we move forward, but the idea is, consider some ideas that are outside of the box! Hopefully we'll learn more ideas from other parents, as well!

So what does all this boil down to?

- Start considering tech rules early.
  - What access does your child have to technology? What rules or limits are appropriate for your household?
- Consider your own behavior and the example that you set.
  - Remember to follow your own household rules.
- Each household is different – what is most important is that your rules work for your household!
- Talk to other parents. What has (or hasn't) worked for them?

 Activity:

Setting household rules should be a family activity! The activities throughout this handbook, when completed, will create a set of household rules for your family. Consider deciding the rules and consequences together - remember, this applies to everyone in the household - and have everyone 'sign' when completed. Household tech rules can and should be revisited at any time as children grow and become more responsible. Many parents say having these household rules posted in their home can help. Check out the next page to start creating your household tech agreement with your family!

Before we begin to create our Family Tech Agreement, we have to know a few things about the tech usage in the household. Having discussions about online activity is critical to online safety, so let's start here!

Who uses tech in the household?

1.______________________   4.______________________

2.______________________   5.______________________

3.______________________   6.______________________

    Additional:____

What connected devices are there in the household? This may be computers, cell phones, laptops, tablets, televisions, gaming systems, smart speaker devices, connected appliances, smartwatches, fitness trackers, or others!

List of devices to consider:

____

____

____

____

How do the members of the household use the devices listed above?

- ☐ Work
- ☐ School/Homework
- ☐ Making calls
- ☐ Texting/Messaging
- ☐ Taking photos
- ☐ Shopping
- ☐ Listening to music/books/podcasts
- ☐ Creating content (videos, live-streaming)
- ☐ Gaming/Online gaming
- ☐ Social media
- ☐ Health/Fitness/Exercise
- ☐ Watching videos/streaming
- ☐ Reading
- ☐ Watching TV
- ☐ Learning
- ☐ Other: ______________________________________

What does each person from the household list above say is their favorite online activity? (Numbers should correspond with the list above).

1.______________________   4.______________________

2.______________________   5.______________________

3.______________________   6.______________________

    Additional:____

Chapter 2

Stack 'em up! Building Blocks for Online Safety

I've provided online safety presentations to tens of thousands of parents and child safety professionals, and it's led me to determine a few basic building blocks for online safety. The goal is to get everyone on the same foundational level, and then additional tech information can be sought out or learned, depending on a child's age and the family's needs.

My other goal with this foundational approach is to provide people with easy-action items that don't require much effort and actually do increase their household's online safety! There's nothing worse than learning about something you think is important, and then having a number of items added to your to-do list to research, purchase, or set up in order to get started with said-important topic. I think this approach makes it overwhelming and undermines our confidence. We've already set the stage for our easy-action items in Chapter 1, so it will come as no surprise – the key to these building blocks is to set rules that work for your household and *stick to them!* You may read recommendations by different organizations for appropriate screen time amounts, appropriate tech rules, and appropriate online usage and interactions, but they all vary. Here's why: *every household is different.* No screens after 8 PM may work for your family, but may be unrealistic for my family. If 9 PM is what my household agrees is appropriate, the important takeaway is that we set *and stick to* that 9 PM screen limit. These rules will likely be more difficult for us as parents and guardians to adjust to than for our children! I recently heard from some parents that were laughing because they were indicating to their child that it was time to put away the screens for the night, and the child asked, "Is it 9:30 already?" The parents couldn't remember if they had set the time at 9 or 9:30! They had to find a way to answer without showing they'd forgotten. I laughed out loud considering how easily that situation could happen – yet another reason that keeping a list of the house rules posted can be useful to us!

Now, onto our building blocks.

Let's get started!

1. Utilize parental approvals and device settings
2. Set screen times and zones
3. Have discussions early and often

Utilize parental approvals and device settings

This, admittedly, is my step with the most 'effort' when it comes to knowing or understanding technology. I am not an avid tech user, and even as someone who worked with tech and tech safety every single day for years, I'm terrifically clueless sometimes when it comes to knowing how things work. I say that so you understand that it's okay to be overwhelmed! Your favorite search engine is your friend in this instance (and many others, really!) and can usually provide you with information or steps to get you what you need. Google Help and Apple Support can be extremely helpful tools, as well. I've referenced both of them for their Family Link and Family Sharing information many times. And if you don't know how to access them (you aren't alone, I can't remember it, either), you can search any of these terms in Google or your search engine: Google Help, Google Support, Google Family, Apple Help/Support, Apple Family, Parental Controls – they all get you to the right links to help you set up this great feature.

How do parental controls help? Parental controls refer to a group of settings that help you manage your child's device(s), account(s), and apps. Family Link (Google) and Family Sharing (Apple) can be set up to place limits on screen times, manage accounts and data settings, and even see locations of a child's device. Accounts can be set for certain age levels, which in turn sets limits on items rated as containing explicit content, prevents certain web content, and can restrict some search content, as well. Lastly, the parental controls and approvals assist with app management. These are all great features, but the app management can be very useful in conjunction with the other building blocks for ongoing safety in the household. If the child is interested in downloading a game or app, it sends a notification to the parent linked to that account. This provides a few benefits:

- You know what apps or games they're using! This can be incorporated into discussions about their interests and activities.

- You can learn more about what apps or games they're interested in. Doing a search of that app or game can inform you of benefits, risks, and options for consideration. You can then use the information you find to help set the boundaries of use with your child if you approve the download.
  - General search engine searches can provide some information, but Google Play and iTunes can provide great summaries, as well!
  - Another great resource for learning about apps and games is Common Sense Media (commonsensemedia.org). You can look up the app or game and access information including summaries and safety considerations. They also include parent and child reviews, so you can see more information about experiences others have had. Lastly, there are discussion starters included, helping to provide ways to approach safety information with your kids about those specific apps or games. Common Sense has put limits on how many free searches you can do in a month, but it's a good resource to be aware of.
- The opportunity to learn more about the app or game then provides an opening to discuss the app or game with your child before you approve it (if you plan to approve it). You can also make choices about what the user settings or privacy settings will need to be for their use.
  - Bonus: You can also set time limits for usage within certain apps!

Privacy settings can be a valuable tool, as well. Your child may be old enough, mature enough, or responsible enough that parental approvals might be unnecessary or overbearing. If you have used parental approvals for younger children, they can 'graduate' to privacy settings-only instead. If you did not use parental approvals for your child when they were younger, you may find that more frequent reviews of privacy settings might be needed, or more restrictive setting choices could be considered.

How can privacy settings help? Privacy settings can manage two main things: the information that the app accesses *from* a user and the information that the user *shares*. Apps ask for certain permissions, such as permission to access location, contacts, camera, or microphone. Privacy settings also allow for certain account settings, such as age of user, who they can communicate with or who can communicate with them, who they can be friends with or who can request to be a friend, and more. Privacy settings should be reviewed upon initial download and should also be reviewed regularly. Privacy settings may need to change as the child gets older and more responsible in their tech use. Default privacy settings can also change when apps are updated, providing a great reason for regular review and discussion!

If you are anything like me, this will also help you remember to check your own privacy settings, something we all should be doing regularly! If this section brings to mind what age a user chooses when they create an account, that topic is discussed more in depth in Chapter 4.

Set screen times and zones

Screen time limits:

This idea was introduced in Chapter 1, but let's dig in. We all know that attention to screen time is important. Thoughts on how levels of screen time impact mental health have changed over years, with a recent focus on quality of screen time vs quantity of screen time. However, something that has been well-proven is the impact of screens on sleep, and it's easy to see the impact on physical activity as well. This makes it an easy decision to create limits on our children's screen time.

As a reminder, there is no 'right' rule for screen time! There are guidelines out there from the American Academy of Pediatrics, the World Health Organization, the Centers for Disease Control and Prevention, and more to help provide you with ideas for appropriate screen time amounts, but you decide what's best for your household. However, as you navigate parenting, keep online usage in mind with all aspects of parenting. If your child is struggling with tiredness, short patience, and grumpy attitude, you might be thinking that you need to change their bedtime. That might be the case, but you might also need to make sure that they're getting a break from screens before bedtime and certainly that they are getting a break from screen time throughout the night. Our children need quality sleep for healthy development!

So, let's discuss screen time limits. In Chapter 1, this idea was introduced in terms of a number of videos or shows a child could watch in a day. Another option for younger children is to use actual limits of time (15 minutes a day, 20 minutes a day, etc) and have an actual timer that kids can use. Parental control features on the devices can also help with screen time, as can additional apps for parental monitoring that can be downloaded. Some allow for additional screen time to be added or 'earned,' so take a look at the built-in tools or free/purchased apps that will be the best fit for your household needs. The resource section at the end of this handbook explains how to find app options. Another parent provided this idea that I adore: her kids always have one offline activity or hobby they're involved in. What a great way to make sure that they are enjoying whatever they're taking a screen time break to do! And since you can see them doing it, it also gives a way for you to interact with your child on that activity of interest, be it sports, art, woodworking, legos, crocheting/knitting, biking, skating, gardening, sewing, and the list goes on and on! It's very possible that the online and offline hobbies will also intersect, with some online research being done to help further the offline interest.

As alluded to earlier, screen time limits might also be appropriate to set for certain times of the day. "No screens after 8 PM," or "No screens at the dinner table," are popular options I hear. Another suggestion I've heard that I try to follow at home is one screen at a time. Think about times when the TV is on while you are answering emails or on Facebook. You definitely aren't paying attention to both, you certainly limit your in-person interactions, and it sets an example for kids on tech use. It's a tough habit to break, but I'm always glad when I purposely make the choice to focus on one screen or task at a time. Additionally, end-of-day screen time limits are great ways to ensure that our kids get those much-needed breaks from the screens, and hopefully provide us with some uninterrupted time to interact with family, as well. This can be a tough one for older family members or adults to comply with! While older-aged children might have different end-of-day limits (and please don't think I'm indicating that parents have to follow these rules once all the kids are in bed), there are probably rules everyone should stick to if agreed upon, such as the dinner table rule example. If a parent needs an "unless it's a work call" exception, that can be explained.

You might also have a child that doesn't adhere to the rules. Perhaps you've set a rule for no screens after 9 PM, but you don't check at night and later find that your child is checking or using their phone in their room late at night. If the device is in the child's room with them overnight, it will be very difficult to resist the urge to use or check it at some point. For phones, a great idea is to have a charging station somewhere in the house overnight, for instance, the kitchen counter. If your child is sneaking out to grab their phone from the charger at night, then the charging station might need to move to the parent's bedroom.

I've also spoken with parents that have set time limits on their internet through their router. If you didn't know this was an option, I'll confess that I also wasn't aware of it and didn't know how to do it, but a quick search online showed me that routers usually have parental controls, as well, which includes a setting for scheduling the network. If I need to remove internet access overnight at any point, I'm keeping this option in my pocket!

Screen zone limits:

This is one of my favorites, and is more geared to parents of older children or teens. Very similar to screen time limits, it recognizes that there is heightened risk for poor decision making when there is less supervision over electronics. How many of you are remembering having your computer in the family room as a child? (*I'm raising my hand*). How about a corded phone in a common area or having to keep the cordless phone in the family room when you talk? (*Raising my hand on these, too*). This is the same idea!

A large amount of self-generated nude images that teens take are taken in the bathroom. If we remove it as an option, it will reduce the opportunity to take or send those photos! A simple rule of "No phones in the bathroom" will go a long way toward reducing online child exploitation reports on some of the common platforms: Snapchat, Instagram, Facebook, Google, etc. And remember, these are household rules, so this might be another tough habit for parents to break, but well worth it! Similarly, if there's a way to have a "No devices in the bedrooms" rule, that's great! I recognize that this one is pretty unrealistic, so let's bounce that bar down a couple of notches. How about a "No devices behind closed doors" rule? Or, "No phones/camera devices behind closed doors?" Again, the rule can be what best fits your household, but it is important to note that there are many reasons that teens and tweens take risky photos of themselves, the more common ones including for romantic/dating reasons and because of peer pressure. Peer pressure can be difficult on anyone, let alone children. If we remove the opportunity to agree to the request (i.e., "I can't, my mom can literally see me right now"), we can help them to respond to the peer pressure appropriately. Some home layouts might not make a difference if doors are open, so determine a rule that helps in your household and is appropriate for your child's age and adjust as needed.

*A quick note before we leave this section. We'll talk more about peer pressure and sexting in Chapter 5, but it's important to note here that these pressures may be facing our children before we expect them. It was not uncommon in my ICAC experience to see children in 4th or 5th grade being exposed to peer pressure to sext (and to see children sexting, whether or not they understood what they were doing), so please, find an age-appropriate way to talk with your child about what they're doing online before you think you need to, and let them know that no matter what's happened, they can always come to you for help if they need it.

Having discussions early and often

I hope that this is the easiest of the suggestions I provide throughout this handbook! However, I understand that the topic of online activities, online safety, and technology in general can be daunting. Here's what I can offer:

- Kids know technology better than we do. This isn't going to change, and we shouldn't pretend things are any different! We know the safety side, so be confident in the fact that you know there *are* things to be concerned about, and that the main goal is talking with them about their online activity.

- Let them teach you! Letting kids teach us technology is probably the best way to learn it and it's a win-win! It helps build their confidence, and it starts the conversation (which is the goal).
- The more we do it, the easier it is. You don't have to know the ins and outs of technology; you just have to talk to your kids about what they are doing online so you are aware.

Bonus: The more aware we are of what they like to do online, the easier it is to have relevant conversations about their online activity.

- The goal is to break down barriers and set yourself up as their trusted adult. If you are regularly talking about online activity, you will be an obvious resource if they need help!

If those reasons aren't enough, try this one on for size:

Having FREQUENT CONVERSATIONS with your child about their online activity has the BIGGEST INFLUENCE ON CHANGE in their online behavior.

This harkens back to the very beginning of this handbook. Do all of our conversations need to be painful and lengthy? Absolutely not! The goal is just to include our kids' online activity in our discussions about their lives. Our children's online and offline lives are integrated, and not able to be referred to separately as they could in the past. When we see red flags and are trying to figure out a reason, we should consider both online and offline perspectives. When we discuss their interests or their day's activities, we should include their online activities and interests, as well as what happened at school or as part of extracurricular activities. These conversations will naturally evolve into what they need to: discussions about online use, appropriate activity, responsible digital citizenship, safety, and most importantly – what to do if they need help. One of my favorite suggestions around this topic is to set up an icebreaker plan with your child(ren). If they need to talk about something but think you might get angry, they can text you, send a certain emoji/bitmoji, email you – whatever you determine together. It lets you know that a conversation is coming and you can prepare yourself to hold your emotions in check (hopefully!) while you listen and figure out a solution with your child. I've also heard suggestions of a notecard placed somewhere in the house. If the child needs to have a serious discussion or needs help, they can bring the notecard to you and know that you'll listen.

The earlier we can start these conversations, the better. They will be easier conversations, and will evolve as a child's use of technology evolves (because we'll be aware of what they're doing)! With young children, you can talk about what they like about the game or app or what they don't like about the game or app, and see where the conversation goes. To broach online safety topics, consider easy topics like what to do if a pop-up comes on the screen; eventually this will lead to talking about oversharing.

Another great option for discussions for young children is to teach them what to do. Empower them to be able to take action if needed, and this will build confidence and will also grow with them as their tech use evolves. This could include teaching them to turn off the screen, hit the back button, turn the device off altogether, or just hand the device to a parent for help. As they get older, actions might include how to report behavior in an app or game, or how to block someone.

Coming from an ICAC perspective, I always have to consider things in terms of online exploitation, and that's a tough thing to explain at any age! My favorite way to include this for young ages when needed is to use, "If something makes you feel funny, you can…(fill in the blank with an action item)." Everyone understands that, and it can cover a lot of bases, from unwanted communication to unexpected Google search results.

It's crucial to remember two things.

1) Technology is incredibly beneficial! It's easy to become overwhelmed by safety concerns and technology advances, but the social, educational, medical, and business advantages that technology provides us cannot be ignored. We want to teach our children to use technology responsibly while reaping its benefits.
   -AND-

2) That our children aren't doing anything wrong! They are doing the same things that we did as children, such as:

- o   Dressing up dolls → Updating avatars or Bitmojis
- o   Playing with blocks/legos → Roblox or Minecraft, anyone?
- o   Listening to music → It's just different formats!
- o   Passing notes → Texting, messaging

And more! However, they are interacting on a much larger global platform (and with so many more people). It is up to us to help keep them safe as they explore their world and who they are. We all make mistakes; if they make a mistake and need help, they need to know they can always ask for it and that we will always be there.

✍️ Activity:

Let's continue with our Family Tech Agreement! For this section, consider discussing what those basic screen time(s) and screen zone(s) will be for your household. Remember, these are household rules that everyone should agree to.

Activity B: THE ___________________ FAMILY SCREEN TIME CONTRACT

Screen time limits

| | School Nights & Weeknights | Weekends & Holidays |

Devices down at (what time?): ___________________   ___________________
Where do the devices go overnight? ___________________   ___________________
Devices are turned back on after:___________________   ___________________

-OR-

Our family limits screen time on weekends and holidays to _____ hours/minutes per day.

BONUS: Choose one (or more) offline interest, hobby, or activity for each household member.

Name:________________   Interest(s):_____________________________
Name:________________   Interest(s):_____________________________
Name:________________   Interest(s):_____________________________
Name: _______________   Interest(s):_____________________________
Name: _______________   Interest(s):_____________________________

Additional: ____

Screen Time Blackouts

Our family does not use our devices when we have: (check all that apply)

☐ Family meals   ☐ Friends visiting   ☐ Sleepovers
☐ Family gatherings   ☐ Playdates   ☐ Walking or Driving
☐ Other: _________   ☐ Other:_________   ☐ Other:__________

Screen Zone Blackouts

Our family does not use devices in the following rooms or under the following conditions:

☐ Bathrooms   ☐ Bedrooms   ☐ Rooms with closed
☐ Other:_________   ☐ Other:_________   doors

Family Tech Agreement EXCEPTIONS:

____
____

Chapter 3
8 Going on 18: So They Want a Device

 "But Mom, EVERYONE has a phone!" Does this sound familiar? We know that every child does **not** have their own smartphone, but sometimes it seems like it – and the age at which they get them is decreasing. According to Pew Research, nearly one in five parents of a child 11 and under say their child has their own smartphone (Pew Research Center, 2020). Now, I'm going to stick with my 'it's your household' rule on this: There is no right or wrong age answer for a phone, either. You set the rules for your household, you determine what is the right age for your child to have a device. But there are some safety considerations to take into account when considering our children getting phones, and there are questions that we can ask to help us determine if it's right.

Safety Considerations

While there is no right age, there is a notable quote to share. Andrew Yang, the Founder of Humanity Forward, wrote the following:

> "YOU'LL SEE A LOT OF THINGS IN SILICON VALLEY THAT YOU WON'T SEE IN THE REST OF THE COUNTRY. BUT THERE'S ONE THING YOU WON'T SEE THERE THAT'S BECOME COMMONPLACE EVERYWHERE ELSE—CHILDREN ON SMARTPHONES. THE CREATORS OF THE TECHNOLOGIES AND SOCIAL MEDIA APPS THAT ARE DOMINATING AN EVER-ENLARGING PORTION OF OUR CHILDREN'S LIVES ARE OFTEN THE ONES WHO ARE MOST WARY OF GIVING THEIR CHILDREN ACCESS TO THEM."

(From an essay written as part of the 2020 Common Sense research report "Tweens, Teens, Tech, and Mental Health: Coming of Age in an Increasingly Digital, Uncertain, and Unequal World.")

Odgers, C. & Robb, M. B. (2020). Tweens, teens, tech, and mental health: Coming of age in an increasingly digital, uncertain, and unequal world, 2020. San Francisco, CA: Common Sense Media.

I feel it is worthy of attention that the creators of technology and social media are the ones limiting their children's access to it. When we give our children smartphones, we are literally putting a *computer in their pocket*. They can access, communicate, and post anything at any moment. This might mean texts or games with friends, or it might mean communicating with strangers. And as much as we wish it weren't true sometimes, the age-old (in terms of technology, anyway) saying is true: Once posted, always posted. Our children don't always think twice, post once. For goodness' sakes, *adults* don't always think twice, post once! When giving them a smartphone, it is important that they're responsible and recognize when it is and isn't okay to be online and posting: classrooms, locker rooms, events, etc.

The comment I hear most frequently is that the parent needs their child to have a smartphone so that they can see their child's location. It might certainly be the case that this is the right decision for some families – again, your family, your decision – but as with all tech choices, there are benefits and risks. Location services can often be quite convenient, and may even be absolutely necessary in some instances. The risks, however, are that a young child has a connected device and are now potentially sharing their location publicly if/as they post. As mentioned previously, it is important to be aware of the different perspectives so you can weigh out the information and make an appropriate, informed decision.

When is it Right?

We, as guardians, can feel under pressure to make a decision when this milestone of getting a phone is requested by our kids, and we've already talked about the difficulty of making decisions under pressure! Luckily, there are a few questions that you can ask, and discuss with your child, to help them understand what you are looking for from them to show they're ready and the reason for your decision.

- Do they 'check-in' with you if asked? Do they keep up with chores or homework without a lot of reminders?
  - These can be good indicators of responsibility, which is one of the main considerations.
- Do they lose or break things?

- o Smartphones are expensive, there's no way around it. If your child is constantly losing (or breaking) toys, books, homework folders, or other items that aren't of high value, are they ready to be responsible for a pocket-sized computer?
- Can they adhere to limits?
  - o If provided with limits, can they follow them with minimal prompting? Consider the types of rules you'll put in place for the device – classroom or school use, time limits at home – will they follow the rules that come with the device?
- Why do they want it?

  - o Last but not least, why do they want it? This is my favorite question to ask. One parent shared that they asked their child this question, and the child took it very seriously, formulating an actual PowerPoint presentation, complete with research supporting their position. I absolutely loved this! While it may seem a bit overboard, I think there are multiple reasons that this is a good idea. It actually makes them think about why they do want or need that device. It makes them seek out information to support their viewpoint, and they'll likely find safety and risk awareness information at the same time. You might not be interested in pulling out a projector for them, but asking them to put together a proposal of sorts could be a good way to have a more in-depth discussion about this question.

Another great consideration for children's devices is to develop a Device Contract for them. This is similar to the household tech agreement discussed in Chapter 1, and covers more specifics about the device and types of usage. While it can still consider things like screen times and screen zones in the household for usage of that device, it can also focus more specifically on things like app usage and management, how and with whom they can communicate, and how frequently you'll both look at the device together.

If your child already has a device and you are reading this, wishing you had done some of these, it's not too late for setting some rules or boundaries around usage. You may need to tread lightly, but there are ways to come to an agreement on newly-created contracts for already-used devices. Children will sometimes say that they'll pay for the device and then it will be *theirs*, so no rules! I think this is a tricky argument to manage, but it is an argument to be aware of. You could talk about how if they have a phone, they can't use your wifi, can't use the device in your home, or other restrictive rules like that. There's risk in these responses, similar to risk involved with taking devices away as punishment. Kids will always find a way to access devices and the internet, whether it is through a friend's outdated device, through school, the library, or other ways. Remember, the goal is to keep open and honest conversations happening about online usage to help guide them in their tech usage as good digital citizens.

A very good analogy is to compare internet safety to learning to drive. We don't throw our children the car keys when they turn 16 and tell them, "Good luck!" We spend an extensive amount of time teaching them the rules of the road, providing supervised practice, setting restrictions for unsupervised driving, and letting them earn more responsibility and trust until they graduate to driving on their own with no restrictions. We can look at tech safety the same way. Before we even give them access to the devices, we should be having discussions about safety and rules. As they start getting older and using technology more independently, the discussions and rules should evolve. And much like if a young driver says they're going out for the night, we should be asking Who? What? When? With going out, we might ask the following:

- Who are you going with and who will be there?
- What will you be doing/where will you be?
- When will you be home?

Online usage should be similar:

- Who are you interacting with/playing with/talking to? Consider what the privacy settings allow for who they can interact with and who can interact with them.

- What are you working on/interested in/playing or doing online? Let them teach you, if possible.
- When will you be done (or what are the screen time limits)?

We should be guiding youth toward using technology responsibly on their own, and building and earning trust is a big part of that equation.

Activity:

If your child doesn't have a device but wants one (or when they do want one), have them create a type of proposal on why they **should have** a device. This can be any format they're interested in: written paper, typed report, presentation, live-action play – encourage them to get creative!

When your household decides a child is ready for a device, or if they already have one, consider a device contract. You can use the options below or create your own!

Why it's the right time for me to have a device:

____

____

____

____

____

Device Contract: Select the appropriate options for your child to review and agree to:

- ☐ I will not text or place phone calls after _______ p.m.
- ☐ I will keep my phone charged at all times.
- ☐ I will answer or respond promptly when my parent/guardian(s) contact me.
- ☐ I will not go over our plan's monthly data usage. If I do, I understand that I may be responsible for paying any additional charges or that I may lose my cell phone privileges.
- ☐ I understand that I am responsible for knowing where my phone is and for keeping it in good condition.
- ☐ I will obey any rules my school has regarding cell phones, such as turning them off during class or keeping them on vibrate while riding the school bus.
- ☐ I will alert my parents when I receive suspicious or alarming messages, phone calls, or texts from people I don't know.
- ☐ I will alert my parents if I am being harassed by someone.
- ☐ I will not send embarrassing photos or videos of my family or friends to others. In addition, I will not use my phone's camera to take embarrassing photos or videos of others.
- ☐ I will not use my device to take inappropriate or explicit images of myself or others.
- ☐ I will not use my phone to buy or download anything without asking permission first.
- ☐ Devices aren't available after school until homework and chores are completed.
- ☐ Our family agrees to review device settings together (how often?): ___________
  - ○ Review and determine device settings, such as location and parental approval.
- ☐ Other:____
- ☐ Other:____

Chapter 4

So They Want Social Media

Children wanting accounts on social media and apps might seem similar to wanting a device, but there is more to consider from this aspect! We already discussed parental approvals of apps and games, but I'll toss it in here as a reminder to be aware of the games and apps that your children use. That may be through parental approvals, through general discussions with your child, or through review of their devices.

Let's say we decided in Chapter 3 to get our child a phone. (Even if we didn't, our children are still able to be active participants in a number of games and apps on other devices, computers, or gaming platforms). If our child now asks to create an account on a specific app (or game), there are a few things to consider:

- What is the minimum age?
  - Many people disregard the age required by apps. For instance, TikTok's minimum age for users is 13, but it's well known that children younger than that are active on TikTok. Even with a parent's awareness or approval, a child misrepresenting their age on an app comes with risks. TikTok's Guardian's Guide specifically states:
    "TikTok is only for those aged at least 13 – or 14 in South Korea and Indonesia – and it's important that your teen provides their real date of birth. From restricting access to certain features to tailoring the ads people can see, accurate information helps ensure community members have the correct age-appropriate experience. For example, in addition to our age requirement, we do not allow younger people on TikTok to use age-restricted features such as the ability to host LIVE or use Direct Messaging." https://www.tiktok.com/safety/en/guardians-guide/

This sums up the concerns really well and should be considered across all apps and user experiences. If a child user is putting in a false age to make themselves appear old enough to meet the app's age requirements, they are experiencing content that is deemed appropriate for older users. For instance, if I'm 8 years old and create a Facebook account that says I'm 13, I'm receiving content filtered for 13-year-olds by the app. When I actually do turn 13, the app now thinks that I'm 18. Not only will content no longer be filtered to remove violent, sexual, political,

---

"...if I'm 8 years old and create a Facebook account that says I'm 13, I'm receiving content filtered for 13 year olds by the app. When I actually do turn 13, the app now thinks that I'm 18."

---

or other adult-context content, but the app will also try to connect me with other users as though I'm an 18-year-old. Not to mention, many of the apps now either have a dating component or a feature to try to 'make new friends.' As 13-year-old-me is getting connected online with adults of all ages, we can see the importance of real ages on our children's accounts.

For those of you scoffing at Facebook no longer being popular with kids, I would note that Facebook is one of the largest ICAC CyberTip reporters, and that we often saw young users being exploited in those reports. Predators go where children go, and if they see young or vulnerable users on an unpopular app, it being unpopular won't stop them from preying on our children.

Privacy concerns are also something to understand. The

Children's Online Privacy Protection Rule, or COPPA, imposes certain requirements on websites or online services with users under 13 to help reduce collection

of children's personal information. As you are downloading free apps or games, remember: In technology, if something is free, it's probably because *you* are the product. They're collecting data on everything that you do, and this is a good time to consider what permissions you've provided the app upon downloaded or signing up for it.

Lastly, misrepresenting your age is usually a violation of the agreed upon terms and conditions of the app or site. While that may not seem overly concerning to you, this brings back to mind earlier topics and the example that we're setting for our children with our online use. To the extent that it's possible, we should be at least aware of scope of the terms and conditions we are agreeing to and we should be setting the example that, if the app requires a certain age level for safety reasons, that our child cannot have their own account if they haven't yet reached that age.

- What are the features of the app or game?
  Here's an important note for social media and app use when considering online safety. Many parents get snagged on certain 'risky' apps when we want to focus on behavior. While there are certainly apps that are riskier than others, the risk generally lies in the function of the app being used rather than the app itself.

  What do I mean by this? If I don't allow my child to download Risky App A because it has vanishing photos, it's possible my child will download Risky App B, which has vanishing photo capabilities that I didn't realize. Apps are constantly competing, too, so an app your child uses that didn't previously have that capability may now have updated to include that function. Yes, sometimes, you should refuse certain apps based on risk level. But more frequently, you should talk about the risky behavior of concern – focus on the behavior – so that message can carry across any app or device. During one of my years with the ICAC, Pinterest was one of our top CyberTip-reporting Electronic

Service Providers for the year! I would never have thought to talk about online safety and Pinterest in the same sentence. Now, it sums up a very important message of online safety:

FOCUS ON THE BEHAVIOR, NOT THE APP.

Now, let's focus on the idea of the app's features. These may seem obvious to consider: is it a game with violence or adult themes? But let's look further: what is the app popular for? Does it have live-streaming components? If so, it would be good to have boundaries set in place around where our children can live-stream, what they can broadcast, and who can view it. Does it have disappearing or vanishing qualities? Again, this may or may not be something your child is ready for. If and when you decide that it is appropriate, there may need to be specific communication around this.

- Who can communicate with them and who will they be communicating with?

  Many of us grew up with a main message of 'stranger danger,' and while this can still be a high risk, for many people, communicating with strangers online is a common practice. For example, consider online dating. If we're setting examples for healthy and safe internet usage for our children, and then we are online dating and meeting people from an app offline, what type of message are we really sending? They see the examples we're setting, and it's important to own that. Maybe the message is to explain the safety precautions you are taking if you meet someone.

  I'm certainly not condoning our children meeting people in real life that they only know online. But I recognize that in some instances, it happens and they are real kids wanting to hang out with other kids. If this is the case, maybe the rule is that you go along. But let's back up – and set the rule initially on who they can communicate with online.

We can set privacy settings to friends only, we can select that only people with our information can request to be our friend, but these are not failsafe options. We should also be talking to our children about what types of things are safe to talk about online, and what types of things they shouldn't talk about online. We can talk about friends that we know versus friends that we know *of* (perhaps this user is a friend of a friend). But realistically, at some point, they will interact with strangers online and we should set the stage to make that as safe as possible.

A parent once shared with me that they require anyone that their child doesn't know but wants to 'friend them' that they do a video call with her (the parent). This way, she knows if it is actually a child, and her teenager also starts to understand if excuse after excuse is made to *not* call, perhaps there's a reason why and that isn't a good friend option.

Another friend of mine has children that enjoy online gaming, and the rule in their household is that there are no headphones for gaming. That way, they can hear from the other room what's happening in the game. They can step in if chat becomes too adult or inappropriate, or if bullying becomes rampant or any other possible concerns.

- How will they use the app or game? What rules will be in place? This is a great example of why it is helpful to have a heads up that our kids want to download an app or game. It not only gives us time to learn about it and consider our decisions, but it also gives us the opportunity to have specific conversations with our children about rules, risks, and most importantly, what to do if something happens and they need help.

- Privacy settings

  As mentioned above with the COPPA information, privacy settings help us ensure we know what information an app is accessing, such as contacts, microphone, camera, or location. Privacy settings also indicate to the app how we want to present ourselves as a user: age, communication preferences, friend preferences, posted content, and more. It is good practice to review these with your child upon setup, and also to regularly review them to make sure that your chosen settings haven't changed, as well as to make any changes that are needed as your child's use of the app matures (hopefully). Default settings (and app capabilities) can change with updates, so if you go with defaults, it can be even more important to do regular checks of settings.

In the end, this likely comes down to similar questions for getting a device: determining appropriate level of maturity or responsibility, determining how the app or game will be used, and knowing that rules and limits will most likely be followed if set. The age requirements should be considered, though.

I have had parents tell me that they weren't allowing their children to use a certain app, and that they can use it when they become adults. This is a message I recommend using with caution or as a last resort, and I'll reiterate the learning-to-drive analogy; we want to be their safety net as they learn how to use technology and interact online responsibly, and we want to be able to help them if needed. If we "take away the car keys (i.e. an app or device)" until they are an adult and they go straight from zero to sixty, that increases the risk that they might not exhibit responsible behavior. In the end, we come back to the same message every time:

Communication is key.

 Activity:

If your child wants an app or game that you aren't sure about, have them create a type of proposal on why they **should have** it, similar to the new device activity. This can be any format they're interested in: written paper, typed report, presentation, live-action play – encourage them to get creative!

When your household decides a child is ready for social media, consider some additions to the household tech agreement. You can use the options below or create your own!

Our family agrees that the following apps, social media sites, and/or online games are approved for household use:

______________________________   ______________________________
Username:_____________________   Username:_____________________

______________________________   ______________________________
Username:_____________________   Username:_____________________

______________________________   ______________________________
Username:_____________________   Username:_____________________

Others:________________________   Others:________________________

Social Media Contract: Select the appropriate options for your child to review and agree to:

- ☐ Our family agrees to use Family Link / Family Sharing with parental approvals.
- ☐ Parent/guardian(s) will keep records of all accounts and passwords. Phone/account checks will occur (how often?):____________________
- ☐ Our family agrees to review app privacy settings together: (how often?) _________ *Review privacy settings together regularly.
- ☐ Our family agrees never to use social media to be hurtful or mean to others.
- ☐ I agree not to be a bystander to cyberbullying.
- ☐ I agree to only communicate with people I know or receive parental approval to communicate with others.
- ☐ I agree not to share my passwords with anyone other than my parent/guardian(s).
- ☐ I agree not to post sexualized images.
- ☐ I agree not to overshare personal information, including my current location or schedule.
- ☐ I agree to immediately tell an adult family member if I ever receive any threatening or sexual messages or images.
- ☐ I acknowledge that everything I put online is permanently available, even if it can be immediately deleted or hidden.
- ☐ Other:____
- ☐ Other:____

A lot of online safety information can be grouped under the heading of 'oversharing.' For me, this idea connects the different online exploitation risks and, in a way, oversharing can apply to each from a safety perspective. Online exploitation risks include:

- Thinking twice, posting once
- Online threats
- Hoaxes
- Misrepresenting selves
- Cyberbullying
- Inappropriate chat, images, requests
- Sexting and sextortion
- Online predators

This list might seem overwhelming, or even downright panic-inducing.

"Don't panic!"

Don't panic! I can't say it enough, we must always remember that technology provides us with incredible benefits! Our children, and all of us, are profiting from tech in so many ways. With that in mind, try not to be overwhelmed; you are already taking a huge step to make your home safer by seeking out resources and by having discussions with your kids. Now let's break down the risks.

- Thinking twice, posting once
  - This is a great rule to use when our kids start using social media and start interacting online. I've also heard this referred to as the 'Grandmother Rule': If you wouldn't want your grandmother to see it, don't post it. As mentioned earlier, this is a rule that I think many adults tend to forget sometimes, and we would all do well to consider it in our online interactions. For

children, this can apply to anything: personal information, private/risky photos, bullying comments, inappropriate comments or threats, and more.

- Online threats and hoaxes

In recent years, it isn't uncommon for us to hear about a bomb threat or threat of violence made toward a school. Usually, these are threats and nothing more, but of course they must be taken seriously because they are sometimes acted upon. Sometimes, they are disgruntled students that posted the threat out of anger or frustration but didn't mean it and didn't think twice before they posted. This is a waste of tremendous resources when law enforcement and schools have to consider these threats as valid. It can also have extreme consequences on someone's future, including years of prison time. This is a perfect example of the need to think twice, post once. It's also a great example of oversharing; if you are frustrated, consider reaching out to a trusted person in your life to vent instead of posting emotionally.

- Misrepresenting selves

One of the ways bullying takes place is through misrepresentation online, either by the bully pretending to be someone they aren't and then bullying the victim, or by the bully creating an account to make them look like the victim and then posting maliciously from the "victim's" account. In terms of what to do, this is absolutely a violation of the agreed upon terms and conditions of an app or site and should be reported as abuse of the site. Reporting abuse to the app or site makes them aware of the problem and allows them to take action on the offending person or account. It also provides an opportunity to stop the abuse if it's happening to other online users.

First and foremost, we want our kids coming to us if they need help, but teaching them to report abuse on the app or site can be a great tool when they're ready for it!

- Cyberbullying

    Cyberbullying is like the in-person bullying that has been around for ages, but with a few differences. It can be spread widely with a single click, making it easier to bully. It also follows the victim home into their safe space, which can result in almost-constant bullying with 24/7 access as the child tries to respond to or stop the bullying. Lastly, anonymity adds a new dimension to bullying. The bullying can be anonymous if the bully misrepresents themselves through another's account or if they make efforts to be anonymous, resulting in additional pressure on the child as they are left wondering who is actually saying these things as they interact with people in their lives. Anonymity also comes into play in terms of **disinhibition effect**. We feel safer behind our screens and are more likely to post or say things online that we would not consider doing or saying in person.

    DISINHIBITION EFFECT: "PEOPLE MAY BEHAVE ONLINE IN WAYS THAT APPEAR QUITE UNINHIBITED AS COMPARED WITH THEIR USUAL OFFLINE BEHAVIOR."

    Suler, J. (2005). The online disinhibition effect. International Journal of Applied Psychoanalytic Studies, 2(2).

    This applies to general behavior of tech users, and also to the toxic and damaging behavior of bullies or online predators. Responding to cyberbullying is very difficult. It often doesn't rise to the level of law enforcement response, and families are left unsure of where to go for help. If it happens outside of school, but it might be on a school device (or vice versa), does the school need to be involved? The best advice I can offer is to empower the child and involve them in determining the response, to the extent possible. Bullying creates a power imbalance; letting the child help determine a response can help restore some of that power, as well as ensure that we, as guardians, don't unknowingly make something worse with our response.

We should do our best to teach our children not to be bystanders to cyberbullying, to ask for help if they or someone they know needs help, and last but perhaps most important – not to be a bully. Don't use the "like" button for hate.

- Online predators

  Online predators can be cyberbullies, trolls, and scammers, but in terms of online safety for children, we are referring to individuals seeking to manipulate and exploit children for sexual images or sexual content, or worse, looking to meet a child in real life for sexual purposes. As mentioned previously, we've always provided our children with the message that they shouldn't talk to strangers and even more importantly, not to meet people they don't know in real life. Some of our children will communicate with strangers online, and it may be with or without their guardian's knowledge. Since we are talking to our children about appropriate and inappropriate behavior, hopefully that carries over into the conversations they are having online and keeping them from oversharing. We also hope that our discussions have instilled them with the confidence to say, "No" to anything that seems inappropriate or even just a bit 'off,' and to let us know if they need help - ever.

When sharing online predator red flags and risk factors with kids, we often see kids tune out with the reasoning that they already know this information, and they're smart enough that they wouldn't fall for grooming. If you've tuned out....*listen up.* I've worked in online safety and law enforcement for a long time. I'm generally distrustful of people's motives, I'm sometimes cynical, I'm a confident individual...and sometimes when I read grooming conversations that are reported, I think,

Does that frighten you as much as it frightened me when I realized it? It's because online predators are good at what they do. They practice tactics until they work, and if something doesn't work, they move on to another victim and another tactic. So instead of telling kids about the red flags that *they* should recognize, I often try taking a roundabout route and explain that I know and am glad that they won't fall for these things, but there might be a friend or younger sibling that doesn't know better and that they can catch the red flags for and step in to help.

Grooming isn't a new concept to any of us, but grooming has started to have a slightly different look. We now see some grooming taking place with in-app rewards and purchases, online payments, Amazon wish list purchases, gift cards, and that sort of non-tangible incentive. It also isn't far-fetched to have concerns about grooming by gifting a device; we are all connected through so many devices in our home (phones, computers, TVs, appliances, laptops, gaming devices, and more), it's possible that a child could be using another device to communicate without a guardian's immediate knowledge. Utilizing some of the foundational online safety building blocks and coming up with household rules can help to mitigate chances of this sort of risk happening, or at least going unnoticed. And in the end, our conversations with our children should always be indicating that they can ask for help, no matter what.

- Sexting and Sextortion

    I've combined these two, but they are – or can be – incredibly different risks. Sexting is becoming, not necessarily more  normalized, but *perceived* as more normalized. In my mind, these are still separate ideas, but they are definitely on the same slope. In surveys done of teens, the majority will still say that they have not sent a sexting image. In those same surveys, a higher percentage of teens will say that they think it's 'normal' for their peers to engage in this activity. The stats depend on where you look, and they certainly may be skewed based on how willing teenagers are to admit to the behavior in a written survey, but the increase in perception remains. And let's face it – sexting *is* becoming more common. Youth might do it out of curiosity, out of love, because they're faced with peer pressure, or some other reason, but the end result is the same: as soon as an image is shared, you no longer have control over it. Hence, our think twice, post once rule! Also, the time to decide if you will ever send an explicit image or video is long before you are asked. If you aren't prepared the "ask" and the pressure, it is difficult to handle that pressure. I recommend talking to your child and helping them determine ways or "practice" how they can respond if something like this happens. A part of the problem is that nobody wants to mistrust a friend or significant other. Nobody wants to think that a trusted person would share their content without their consent, but we see it happen quite frequently. The next bullet point on Inappropriate Requests digs into this more deeply, but let's share the message that if someone trusts you enough to share personal content with you, honor that trust! Even if the relationship changes, consider putting yourself in their shoes and making the right decision.

And sending sexual images can, unfortunately, increase the risk of being sextorted. This certainly doesn't mean that sexting leads to sextortion or that sextortion only happens after sexting, but existence of images does increase the risk.

Sextortion is using a person's sexual image or content to threaten and coerce them, usually into sending more sexual content, paying money, or engaging in sexual activity. Perpetrators threaten to post the nude images to friends, family, or school, or may threaten to post it publicly online. Perpetrators also sometimes threaten violence or harm to the victim or victim's family. It's a terrifying trend that has developed in the online safety realm, and can be very impactful on our children. Even though it is never a child's fault if they are manipulated or tricked, child victims may be blamed, or may face shame or embarrassment as part of asking for help. They may also face long-term consequences of being a victim of sextortion, and we should give them all the help and support we can.

More commonly, teenage males are becoming the victims of financial sextortion, with demands that they pay large sums of  money to the perpetrator. These conversations usually involve the perpetrator pretending to be a female to entice online sexual activity or sharing of images, and the conversations and sextortion progress very quickly. Oftentimes, even after complying with demands, the threat will be carried out, and the sextortion will continue. Tragically, there have also been instances where teenagers have committed suicide as a result of sextortion.

Our key message with sextortion (or any safety concern)? You can *always* ask for help. No matter what has taken place, no matter what time of day, you can ask for help and you *can get through it.* There are resources to help, including the ICAC Task

Forces (icactaskforce.org), Thorn (stopsextortion.com), NCMEC (missingkids.org) and more.

- Inappropriate chat, images, or requests

    These last three categories are interwoven, but the topic of inappropriate requests deserves its own heading. Remember the disinhibition effect introduced earlier? I am quite sure that it applies here, as well – to what people think it is okay to request or send online without consent. I've read so many reported chats sent to children with inappropriate requests in them that I've long ago lost count, yet it still surprises me how quickly nude images are asked for from strangers – strangers that are kids! - sometimes. In apps where the intention is 'meeting new friends,' I often read things along the lines of:

    "Hey, thanks for adding me."

    "Sure. What's up?"

    "Trade?"

    [*or other similar question, indicating trading nude*

    Literally the next statement after saying hello to someone! Can you imagine the audacity to feel like it's an acceptable meet-and-greet to ask someone to send a naked picture of themselves? And it always seemed like a toss-up whether the response was telling the requestor to 'buzz off' (or the teenage equivalent) or whether the response *was* to trade images.

So why am I sharing this? I just got done stating how important it is that we don't panic at the idea of online safety and our teenagers, and then share information that is somewhat panic-inducing. I share this information because it's happening. And I think that it's equally important as saying to think twice before you send that we also say...don't ask. Don't ask for personal images. And if someone trusts you enough to share one, don't reshare it! It is a gross violation of trust to reshare someone's personal content without their consent. And don't send unsolicited nude photos of yourself! Not only does the recipient not have a chance to say 'no,' to unsolicited images, running up against the issue of consent again, but it also puts more pressure on them to send their images in return (likely the point). We can help our children deal with this pressure by helping them practice what they'll say if faced with inappropriate requests. Teenagers' brains are still developing, and it makes it extra difficult for them to consider consequences and make appropriate decisions when under pressure, such as peer pressure. If we help them determine responses, they'll be armed with options regardless of the pressure, and more able to make a decision they will be comfortable with long-term.

All of these categories and risks can be frightening and overwhelming, but as we talked about in the beginning of this handbook and throughout, it makes it even more important that we remember the benefits of technology. The benefits can certainly outweigh the risks, particularly if we are taking the steps that you are right now to start the conversation with your children about their online activity. And let's expand the driving analogy: When we are teaching our teens to drive, we don't just show them a bunch of photos of car accidents and then put them behind the wheel. We can consider the same thing for online safety; we don't just tell them about the risks and red flags and then send them online to interact. We, instead, guide them into acting appropriately online, act as mentors and trusted support while they learn, and provide assistance when needed.

✍ Activity:

We can't forget possible consequences in our agreement. This section of the Family Technology Agreement is for determining consequences – together – and for practicing responses. Help your child prepare for difficult situations that *might* happen, and continue to work toward household safety planning to reduce risks.

Our family agrees that breaking this agreement will lead to the following consequences:

____

____

____

____

Practice saying, "No." Parents, complete this section with your child so they can practice responses if they face pressure to respond to something risky, inappropriate, or wrong online. This might include requests for risky images, receiving unsolicited risky images, peer pressure to participate in dangerous social media challenges, or other situations where your teen faces pressure.

- o   Idea 1: ____
- o   Idea 2: ____
- o   Idea 3: ____

Icebreaker

Create an "icebreaker" for difficult conversations.

If someone needs to have a difficult conversation in our family, they can:

- ☐   Text parent/guardian
    - o   the following emoji or message can be used:_______________________________
- ☐   Email parent/guardian
- ☐   Get the identified "We need to talk" notecard
- ☐   Other ideas:

____

____

____

You can always ask for help.

- ☐   I agree that, no matter the situation or what has happened, if I need help, I will tell my parent/guardian or another trusted adult immediately. I acknowledge that I will never think it's too late (too far into a situation or too late at night) to ask for help.

We all make mistakes. It's silly for us to think that our kids won't make them, too. And if they come to us asking for help because they did  something they shouldn't online…that's all it is. It's a mistake. And we can help them! But (and trust me, I know this is easier said than done) we have to do our best to respond without bringing emotion into the picture. We will, undoubtedly, be angry. Angry that our child did something we told them was unsafe and that they shouldn't do, angry at whatever online predator or bully or scumbag interacted negatively with our child, angry at the EXISTENCE OF THE INTERNET! However, save the anger for behind closed doors if possible, and listen to your child as they come to you for help in their time of need. If it helps, remember the ice breaker idea from Chapter 2! Next steps after disclosure might be obvious depending on the situation, but if they aren't, involve your child in the decision-making process. We may overlook something important to them as part of the safety planning or next steps.

The other part of this to keep in mind is the consequences. If our child is the victim of someone sharing their personal image, cyberbullying, sextortion, or other online safety incidents, they will likely have plenty of consequences without us even considering at-home punishment. They'll be facing social consequences (blame, shame, embarrassment) with their peers - even though we know that the victim isn't to blame, it still happens. They may face personal consequences if friendships or relationships end. They may face future consequences if an image is shared or posted, and they don't know how to gain control of that situation or who might see it…forever. Online exploitation can be incredible impactful on victims and families, so in short, cut yourself some slack if you are worried about how to carry out consequences at home. Your family may have agreed upon certain consequences for breaking online rules, but perhaps a conversation about the situation will help to determine a better current response.

I've also had parents tell me regularly that they plan to take away devices as punishment. There may be times where this is completely appropriate! However, as a general recommendation, I would urge you to consider other options instead. Taking away technology will not keep our kids off the internet. They're just going to be sneaky about their access, through a friend's old device, through the library, through school – there are plenty of options for them to connect. However, if they are hiding their online use, we no longer have the option to be involved in what they are doing, who they are talking to, and just checking in on their online lives. But remember – every household is different. You decide what is appropriate and necessary for rules and consequences in your home.

As we reach the end of the handbook, you might be feeling overwhelmed at the idea of remembering the information and keeping up with new technology. Just remember – kids know the tech, but we know the safety side! And you can utilize your kids (and your kids' friends' parents) to help keep up with what's popular.

You've taken a huge step in seeking out online safety information! Take a moment to give yourself a pat on the back, as we should grab them whenever we can. The end of this chapter provides resources, additional information, and tools that might come in useful as you continue to build on your foundational online safety blocks.

Thanks for starting the conversation!

<u>**Resource Ideas & Tools to Use:**</u>

Common Sense Media (commonsensemedia.org)

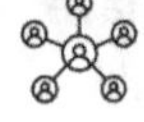 Common Sense Media is a great parent resource. App reviews are available that provide summaries of apps, ratings based on safety information, and both parent and child reviews of apps to help share experiences. The app reviews also provide ratings of different areas of risky content, including language, violence, sexual content, drugs/alcohol use, and more. Lastly, the reviews provide discussion starters for parents and guardians to use while starting online safety conversations with their child(ren).

For online safety professionals, Common Sense offers downloadable, ready-to-use technology safety presentations in a lesson-plan format, with interactive activities to include with presentations.

ConnectSafely (connectsafely.org)

 ConnectSafely is an organization dedicated to educating people about online safety, privacy, security, and digital wellness. Their site includes Parent Guides, Educator Guides, News, and Resources. Resources include guides, pledges/contracts, and podcasts. ConnectSafely also coordinates Safer Internet Day each February for the United States.

Contracts

Much like the Family Technology Agreement created in this book, consider alternate contracts out there for your household needs. There are many templates, examples, or downloadable versions available. They can be located by searching for 'tech agreements' or 'tech contracts' in your favorite search engine. Many of the resources below also have tech agreements and contracts available as resources.

Cyberbullying Research Center (cyberbullying.org)

 The Cyberbullying Research Center has great national statistics and research on cyberbullying, including reports created from youth surveys. Their website shares information on cyberbullying laws, sexting laws, and cyberbullying policies by state.

Device Tools & Features

 Apple – Family Support (apple.com/families)

Google – Family Safety (safety.google/families)

Learn about built-in features on your device(s) for parental controls, child safety, usage, and more! These resources walk through the setup and features available on Family Link and Family Sharing, strong tools to help with parental monitoring of apps and games.

eSafety Commission – Australia (esafety.gov.au)

 The eSafety Commissioner's goal is empowering all Australians to have safer, more positive online experiences. Luckily, the internet doesn't pay attention to country boundaries, and this is great internet safety information that *everyone* can use! This is a great option to consider for regular safety e-newsletters and seeking additional information.

ESRB: Entertainment Software Rating Board (esrb.org)

 ESRB offers explanations of ratings on games (such as E for Everyone), as well as a searchable option to learn more about specific games or apps. There are step-by-step directions for privacy settings on popular gaming consoles in their Tools for Parents section. The section includes a Family Gaming Guide, a user-friendly guide to help manage your kids' gaming experiences.

FOSI: Family Online Safety Institute (fosi.org)

The Family Online Safety Institute is a fantastic option for additional online safety resources. FOSI provides regular safety e-newsletters, templates for technology-use contracts (for different ages), articles, research, and toolkits, with searchable content based on topics or platforms.

Google – Be Internet Awesome & Interland (beinternetawesome.withgoogle.com)

Be Internet Awesome "teaches kids the fundamentals of digital citizenship and safety so they can explore the online world with confidence." The site includes pledges, curriculum, and an interactive online safety game called Interland.

Interland puts key lessons of internet safety into an interactive format that kids enjoy. Users can select from four games, including Kind Kingdom (being kind), Mindful Mountain (oversharing), Tower of Treasure (secure information), and Reality River (fake information).

ICAC Task Force (icactaskforce.org)

The ICAC Task Force is a coordinated national law enforcement network dedicated to investigating, prosecuting and developing effective responses to internet crimes against children. The public facing portion of the website has internet safety information, including links to many resources containing consistent and reliable information. The ICAC website also houses information on where the regional ICAC for each state is located, with links to each Task Force's website.

INEQE Safeguarding Group (ineqe.com)

INEQE are members of the Safeguarding support network in the United Kingdom. While based in Belfast, their online safety information can be of use globally. The Online Safeguarding Hub offers regular e-newsletters, regular short videos to inform users of new apps and trends, and online safety articles and shareables.

National Center for Missing & Exploited Children | NCMEC (missingkids.org)

 The National Center for Missing & Exploited Children has great resources available for starting online safety discussions, including tip sheets and discussion starters.

~Their Resources section includes family resources for healing and support if exploitation has happened to their child.

~The Into The Cloud program is cartoon-episode based and aimed at starting online safety conversations with younger audiences, and additional resources for online safety professionals include downloadable, ready-to-use content for technology safety presentations, along with scripts and videos for audience engagement or sharing.

~NCMEC has created a Take It Down tool for users to submit their under-18 nude images. The tool creates a 'hash,' or a unique fingerprint, for the image, and NCMEC compiles the list of hashes to share with platforms. The images are never uploaded.

~NCMEC also houses the CyberTipline, the reporting tool to report online child exploitation or enticement.

Parental Monitoring Apps

 Some parents and guardians determine that additional parental monitoring is needed beyond Family Link or Family Sharing. There are *many* options, both free and paid, each offering a number of different features. Search for 'parental monitoring apps' in your favorite search engine, or in Google Play or the App Store. Seeking information through a search engine will often give you articles with side-by-side comparisons done of a number of different apps.

Examples of popular features include earning screen time by completing chores, reports of online activity and app usage, monitoring text chat, and even keystroke logging. If you decide to use parental monitoring apps, it is recommended not to hide it from your child. This can harm trust when our goal is to build trust and communciate.

Pew Research Center (pewresearch.org)

Pew has great statistics and research on teens and tech use, including reports created from youth surveys. This information can help provide perspective on youth technology use as parents, guardians, and online professionals determine how to engage in prevention messaging. Online safety professionals may also find this resource useful for statistics for presentations.

THORN (stopsextortion.com)

(parents.thorn.org)

THORN's Stop Sextortion campaign, including their "Cat Video" introduces the topic of sextortion in a more approachable manner that is appropriate for many different audiences. Their website also includes resources focused toward audiences of child victims, parents, professionals, and policy makers, providing support and information regarding incidents of sextortion. For child victims of sextortion that need help, THORN hosts a textline to provide an easier route to access support and/or assistance.

THORN also regularly publishes research on self-generated child sexual abuse material (SG-CSAM) based on youth surveys, information that provides significant perspective for parents, guardians, and child safety professionals.

Activity

Review and sign off on the created agreement from this workbook!

Each family member agrees to follow the contract created in the Family Technology Agreement, Sections A-F, and will review the agreement as a family each year.

SIGNATURES:

1.__________________________ 4.__________________________

2.__________________________ 5.__________________________

3.__________________________ 6.__________________________

Additional:____

____

____

____

____

DATE: ________________________________

www.ingramcontent.com/pod-product-compliance
Lightning Source LLC
Chambersburg PA
CBHW072138150726
48002CB00004B/1530